Pebble® Plus

MEASURING MASTERS

Measuring Time

by Martha E. H. Rustad

PEBBLE

a capstone imprint

Pebble Plus is published by Pebble
1710 Roe Crest Drive, North Mankato,
Minnesota 56003
www.mycapstone.com

Library of Congress Cataloging-in-Publication Data
Library of Congress Cataloging-in-Publication data is available on the Library of Congress website.
ISBN 978-1-9771-0366-6 (library binding)
ISBN 978-1-9771-0551-6 (paperback)
ISBN 978-1-9771-0373-4 (eBook PDF)

Editorial Credits
Michelle Parkin, editor; Elyse White, designer; Heather Mauldin, media researcher;
Laura Manthe, production specialist

Photo Credits
iStockphoto: FatCamera, 19, kate_sept2004, 21, ktaylorg, 5, pick-uppath, 9; Shutterstock: Africa Studio, 15, Halfbottle, cover, IhorL, 13, OlegDoroshin, 11, TinnaPong, 17, TukkataMoji, 7

Design Elements
Shutterstock: DarkPlatypus, cover

Note to Parents and Teachers

The Measuring Masters set supports national curriculum standards for mathematical practice related to measurement and data. This book describes and illustrates how to measure time. The images support early readers in understanding the text. The repetition of words and phrases helps early readers learn new words. This book also introduces early readers to subject-specific vocabulary words, which are defined in the Glossary section. Early readers may need assistance to read some words and to use the Table of Contents, Glossary, Read More, Internet Sites, Critical Thinking Questions, and Index sections of the book.

Printed and bound in China.
970

Table of Contents

Now or Later?. 4

Time Tools 6

How Long Does It Take?. . . .16

Glossary 22
Read More 23
Internet Sites 23
Critical Thinking Questions 24
Index 24

Now or Later?

I'm going to a party.

Here is the invitation.

How long will I have to wait?

We have ways to measure time.

Time Tools

Calendars help us measure time.

Each square is one day.

There are seven days in a week.

There are 365 days in one year.

There are 12 months in one year.

Each month has between

28 and 31 days.

That is about four weeks.

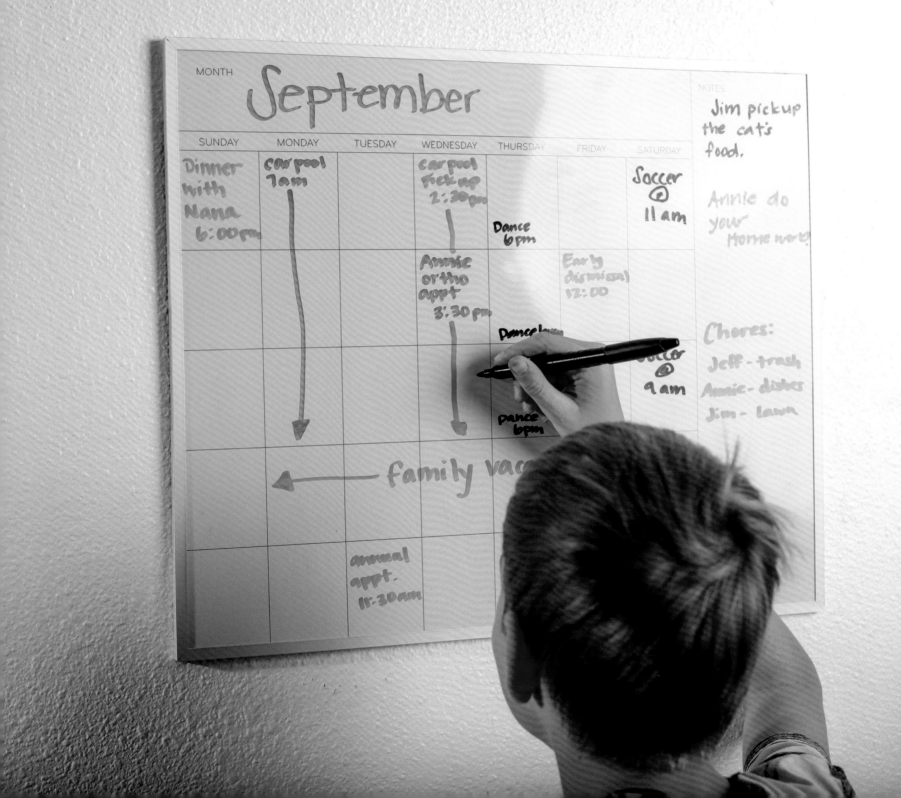

A digital clock shows

hours and minutes.

When the clock shows a.m.,

it is before noon.

When the clock shows p.m.,

it is after noon.

hour

minutes

a.m. or p.m.

An analog clock has three hands.

The short hand points to the hour.

The long hand shows the minutes.

The second hand points to the seconds.

Timers and stopwatches

measure time too.

A timer can count up or down.

We set a timer when we bake a cake.

A stopwatch tells how fast I ran a race.

How Long Does It Take?

Each night I sleep for about 10 hours.

I need lots of rest.

When I wake up, I go to school.

One school day lasts about seven hours.

Soccer practice lasts 60 minutes.

I run across the field in 30 seconds.

I kick the ball into the goal. Score!

The soccer season lasts two months.

I can't wait for the party!

Today is Tuesday. It is 10:00 a.m.

The party is on Saturday at 12:00 p.m.

When does the party start?

In four days and two hours!

Glossary

analog clock (AN-uh-log KLOK)—a clock that has a minute hand, an hour hand, and a second hand to tell the time

calendar (KAL-uhn-dur)—a chart that shows the days, weeks, and months in a year

digital clock (DI-juh-tuhl KLOK)—a clock that shows the time in numbers

invitation (in-vi-TAY-shun)—a letter or card asking someone to come to a party

minute (MIN-it)—a unit to measure time; there are 60 minutes in one hour

second (SEK-uhnd)—a very short unit of time; there are 60 seconds in one minute

timer (TIME-ehr)—a tool that keeps track of time

Read More

Krieg, Katherine. *How Many Hours?* Measuring Time. Mankato, Minn.: Amicus Readers, 2016.

Macdonald, Fiona. *You Wouldn't Want to Live Without Clocks and Calendars!* New York: Franklin Watts, 2016.

Vogel, Julia. *Calendar.* All About Measuring. New York: AV2 by Weigl, 2018.

Internet Sites

Use FactHound to find Internet sites related to this book.

Visit *www.facthound.com*

Just type in 9781977103666 and go.

Super-cool stuff! Check out projects, games and lots more at
www.capstonekids.com

Critical Thinking Questions

1. When is your birthday month? How many days are in that month?

2. What time does your school day start? What time does it end? How many hours are you at school?

3. How many weeks long is your summer break?

Index

a.m., 10, 20

analog clocks, 12

calendars, 6

days, 6, 8, 16, 20

digital clocks, 10

hands, 12

hours, 10, 12, 16

minutes, 10, 12, 18

months, 8, 18

p.m., 10, 20

seconds, 12, 18

stopwatches, 14

timers, 14

years, 6, 8